AaBbCcDdEeFfGgHh

The ABCs of
Oceans

Bobbie Kalman

🌿 Crabtree Publishing Company

www.crabtreebooks.com

A a B b C c D d E e F f G g H h

The ABCs of the Natural World

Created by Bobbie Kalman

For Francine Jarry, a Hawaiian singer,
From a Hawaiian dancer, Mara Makai, (aka Bobbie)

Author and Editor-in-Chief
Bobbie Kalman

Editors
Reagan Miller
Robin Johnson

Photo research
Crystal Sikkens

Design
Bobbie Kalman
Katherine Kantor
Samantha Crabtree (cover)

Production coordinator
Katherine Kantor

Illustrations
Barbara Bedell: pages 8 (left), 9, 11 (shark), 12, 17, 24, 25 (sea star),
31 (dolphin and fish at top right)
Katherine Kantor: pages 10, 11 (skate and elephant fish), 31 (bird, crab, and sea horse)
Jeannette McNaughton-Julich: page 8 (top right)
Trevor Morgan: page 31 (whale)
Bonna Rouse: pages 25 (sea anemone), 31 (all except bird, crab, dolphin,
sea horse, whale, fish at top right, and fish at bottom right)
Margaret Amy Salter: page 31 (fish at bottom right)

Photographs
© Dreamstime.com: back cover, page 21 (top)
© iStockphoto.com: pages 1 (inset), 6 (bottom), 8 (top), 13 (top), 15 (bottom),
21 (bottom), 22 (Queen angelfish at bottom right), 23 (fish at bottom right),
25 (top and sea urchin), 26 (top and bottom), 30 (bottom inset)
© Jez Tryner/SeaPics.com: page 16 (top)
© ShutterStock.com: front cover, pages 1 (background), 3, 4, 5, 8 (bottom), 9, 10, 11,
12, 13 (bottom), 14 (globe), 15 (top), 17, 18 (background), 19 (top left and bottom),
20, 22 (all except Queen angelfish at bottom right), 23 (all except fish at bottom
right), 24, 25 (bottom), 26 (middle), 28 (bottom), 29, 30 (top inset), 31
Other images by Corel and Digital Stock

Library and Archives Canada Cataloguing in Publication

Kalman, Bobbie, 1947-
The ABCs of oceans / Bobbie Kalman.

(The ABCs of the natural world)
Includes index.
ISBN 978-0-7787-3412-3 (bound)
ISBN 978-0-7787-3432-1 (pbk.)

1. Marine animals--Juvenile literature. 2. Ocean--Juvenile literature.
3. English language--Alphabet--Juvenile literature. I. Title. II. Series: ABCs
of the natural world

QL122.2.K34 2007   j591.77   C2007-904239-2

Library of Congress Cataloging-in-Publication Data

Kalman, Bobbie.
The ABCs of oceans / Bobbie Kalman.
p. cm. -- (The ABCs of the natural world)
Includes index.
ISBN-13: 978-0-7787-3412-3 (rlb)
ISBN-10: 0-7787-3412-9 (rlb)
ISBN-13: 978-0-7787-3432-1 (pb)
ISBN-10: 0-7787-3432-3 (pb)
1. Marine animals--Juvenile literature. 2. Marine ecology--
Juvenile literature. 3. Ocean--Juvenile literature. 4. English
language--Alphabet--Juvenile literature. I. Title. II. Series.

QL122.2K353 2007
591.77--dc22
2007026977

Crabtree Publishing Company

www.crabtreebooks.com   1-800-387-7650

Published in Canada
Crabtree Publishing
616 Welland Ave.
St. Catharines, Ontario
L2M 5V6

Published in the United States
Crabtree Publishing
PMB16A
350 Fifth Ave., Suite 3308
New York, NY 10118

Published in the United Kingdom
Crabtree Publishing
White Cross Mills
High Town, Lancaster
LA1 4XS

Published in Australia
Crabtree Publishing
386 Mt. Alexander Rd.
Ascot Vale (Melbourne)
VIC 3032

Contents

About oceans

There are five oceans on Earth. From largest to smallest, they are the Pacific Ocean, the Atlantic Ocean, the Indian Ocean, the Southern Ocean, and the Arctic Ocean. Ocean waters contain a lot of salt. The names of two oceans start with the letter A. Which two oceans are they?

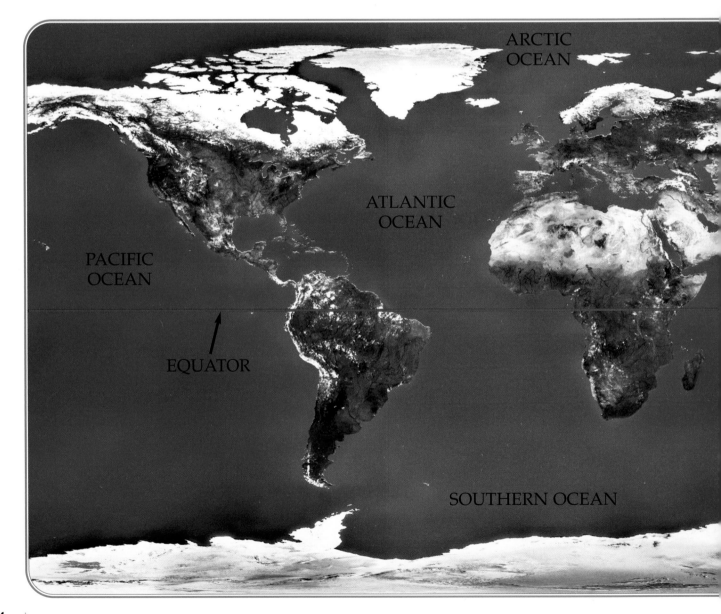

ARCTIC OCEAN

ATLANTIC OCEAN

PACIFIC OCEAN

EQUATOR

SOUTHERN OCEAN

Polar bears swim
in the Arctic Ocean.

PACIFIC
OCEAN

INDIAN
OCEAN

Warm or cold?

There are warm oceans and cold
oceans. The oceans that are close
to the **equator** are warm. The
Indian Ocean is a warm ocean.
The oceans that are far from the
equator are cold. The Arctic
Ocean and the Southern Ocean
are cold oceans.

Warm and cold

The largest oceans have both warm
and cold waters. They have waters
close to the equator and waters
far from the equator. The Pacific
Ocean and the Atlantic Ocean have
both warm and cold waters.

Butterfly fish

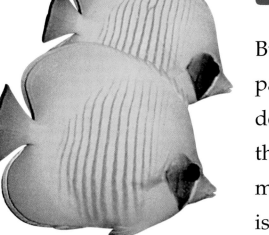

Bluecheek butterfly fish often swim in pairs.

Butterfly fish have bright colors and patterns on their bodies, just as butterflies do. Most butterfly fish have **eye spots** near their tails. Eye spots look like eyes and make it hard to tell where the fish's head is. They fool **predators** and give butterfly fish more time to get away. Predators are animals that hunt other animals for food.

eye spot

Camouflage

Many animals have colors, shapes, or patterns on their bodies that match their surroundings. When animals blend in with their surroundings, they are hidden, or **camouflaged**. Animals are camouflaged so predators will not find them. Predators are also camouflaged so they can surprise the animals they hunt. How is this fish camouflaged in its ocean home?

Dolphins

blowhole

Dolphins are small whales. They are also **mammals**. Mammals that live in oceans need to breathe air above water. Dolphins breathe air through **blowholes**. Blowholes are at the tops of their heads. The black dolphin on the left is called an orca. It is blowing air out of its blowhole. It will then take another breath before going under water.

This Irrawaddy dolphin **calf***, or baby, is swimming close to its mother. The mother and calf come to the surface of the water to breathe.*

EeEeEeEeEeEeEeEeEeEeEe

Eels are fish

fin

Eels are fish with long bodies. Eels have one **fin** along their backs. Fins help fish swim through water. The eel above is a moray eel. It spends most of its day hiding in holes, with just its head sticking out. It waits for fish to come close and then grabs them with its sharp teeth.

This moray eel has the same colors as the animals around it. It is well camouflaged.

9

Fish in oceans

There are many kinds of fish in oceans. All fish are **vertebrates**. Vertebrates are animals that have **backbones** and **skeletons**. A skeleton is made up of all the bones in a fish's body. Not all fish have the same bones. **Bony fish** have hard bones that do not bend.

skeleton   *backbone*

Most fish are bony fish. This lionfish has a backbone and skeleton made of hard bones.

Fish with cartilage

There are some fish that have skeletons made of **cartilage** instead of bones. Cartilage is not hard like bone is. It bends. Your ears are made mostly of cartilage. Sharks and rays are fish that have skeletons made of cartilage instead of hard bones. These fish have very tough skin.

The shovelnose ray above has a skeleton made of cartilage. Rays, sharks, skates, and elephant fish also have cartilage skeletons.

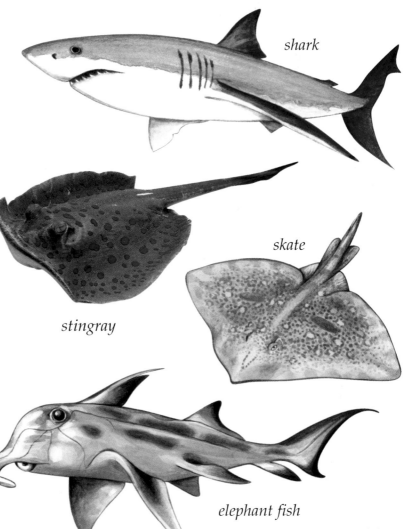

shark

stingray

skate

elephant fish

11

Green sea turtles

*These tiny turtles just **hatched**. To hatch is to come out of an egg. The baby turtles are climbing out of their eggs and their nest.*

Green sea turtles are **reptiles**. They live in oceans. A green sea turtle mother leaves the ocean to lay her eggs on the beach. She digs a nest in the sand and lays her eggs inside the nest. When the sea turtle has finished laying her eggs, she covers the hole with sand. She then returns to the ocean.

Hh Hh Hh Hh Hh Hh Hh

Humpback whales

Humpback whales are huge whales! They live in cold oceans, but they swim to warm oceans to have their babies. The whale on the right is a young whale calf. Male humpback whales **breach**, or leap high out of the water. They also sing beautiful songs. They breach and sing to attract female humpbacks.

This male humpback whale is breaching.

Islands in oceans

AUSTRALIA

An **island** is land that is surrounded by water. Some islands are small, like the island shown below. Some islands are huge. Australia is the largest island on Earth. It has big cities and millions of people.

14

J j J j J j J j J j J j J j J j J j J j J j

Jellies in the sea

Sea jellies have soft bodies that are made mostly of water. Sea jellies have long **tentacles** with stinging parts. They use their tentacles to catch **prey**, such as small fish. Prey are animals that are hunted and eaten by other animals.

*The head of a sea jelly is called a **bell**.*

tentacles

K k K k K k K k K k K k K k

Krait is a sea snake

Kraits are sea snakes. They live both on land and in the ocean, but they can live only in warm oceans. Kraits must breathe air above water. They live in shallow water and search for food in **coral reefs** (see page 23). Kraits are **carnivores**. Carnivores are animals that eat other animals.

L l L l L l L l L l L l L l L l L l L l L l L l

Leafy sea dragons

The leafy sea dragon is not a dragon! It is a fish. This fish is a relative of sea horses, such as the one shown on the right. The leafy sea dragon looks like a bunch of floating seaweed. This disguise fools the animals the fish hunts. The leafy sea dragon eats mainly shrimp. It lives in shallow, warm waters in the Indian Ocean and Pacific Ocean.

sea horse

Many mollusks

Mollusks are animals with soft bodies. They do not have backbones or skeletons inside their bodies. Clams, sea slugs, and octopuses are mollusks. Some mollusks have shells, and others do not. The mollusk below is a nautilus. It has a shell. A nautilus has as many as 90 tentacles. It uses its tentacles to trap prey such as shrimp and small fish.

Nn Nn Nn Nn Nn Nn Nn Nn

Nudibranchs

Nudibranchs are mollusks, too. They are also called sea slugs. Sea slugs are related to garden snails. They move on a strong **foot** the way land snails move. The bright colors of nudibranchs warn predators that these animals taste very bad!

foot

foot ⟵ *land snail*

Octopuses

Octopuses are mollusks, too, but they are much smarter than other mollusks are. Octopuses have good memories, and scientists believe that these animals can also solve problems. Octopuses have eight arms. Each arm has suction cups on its underside. Octopuses use their suction cups to touch, smell, and taste. Octopuses change color to show their moods. What colors are these octopuses?

Porcupine fish

Porcupine fish have **spines** on their bodies, as porcupines do. When a porcupine fish is afraid of being eaten, it swallows a lot of water. Its body becomes round like a ball, and its sharp spines stick out. The spines make the porcupine fish too big and too sharp to eat. Predators stay away from this fish!

Spines are sharp, like needles.

When the porcupine fish is not afraid, its spines lie flat against its body.

21

Queen angelfish

Queen angelfish are beautiful fish. They have tall, thin bodies and brightly colored **scales**. Scales cover and protect the animal's skin. Queen angelfish swim by rowing with their upper and lower fins. They use their tails to turn quickly. Queen angelfish live mainly in coral reefs like this one.

RrRrRrRrRrRrRrRrRr

Reefs full of life

Coral reefs are full of colorful **corals**. Corals look like plants, but they are made up of tiny animals called coral polyps. Coral reefs are found in warm ocean waters near shores. You can see a coral reef in the picture below. Sea turtles, many kinds of fish, and other sea animals live in coral reefs.

corals

Sharks

Sharks are fish with cartilage skeletons. Some sharks are small, but many sharks are big. Big sharks are the **top predators** in oceans. Top predators are not hunted by other animals. Sharks eat many kinds of fish, green sea turtles, octopuses, and other ocean animals. They keep the **populations**, or numbers, of these animals from growing too big.

Tt Tt Tt Tt Tt Tt Tt Tt Tt Tt

Tide pools

Tide pools are found at seashores. Seashores have tides. A tide is the rising and falling of ocean waters. There are two high tides and two low tides every day. At low tide, the water moves away from the shore. Some of the water is trapped among the rocks, forming tide pools. Animals are also trapped there. What animals do you see in the tide pool below?

sea star   *sea anemone*   *sea urchin*

Urchins of the sea

Be careful when you walk on some beaches, or you might step on a sea urchin. Ouch! The shells of sea urchins are covered in sharp spines. The spines help protect sea urchins from predators. Sea urchins can be purple, black, green, or red. These animals are also known as "ocean hedgehogs." Some people think sea urchins look like hedgehogs because hedgehogs also have sharp spines. What do you think?

sea urchin

hedgehog

There are hundreds of purple sea urchins in this tide pool.

26

Volcanoes to islands

An island is land that is surrounded by water. Some islands have formed from **volcanoes**. Volcanoes are cone-shaped mountains with openings, through which hot **lava** pours out. There is red lava pouring out of a volcano on the right. Hawaii is made up of volcanic mountains under the ocean. The parts that rise above the water are the islands of Hawaii.

Some of the volcanoes in Hawaii are still pouring lava into the ocean and forming new land.

27

Worms in oceans

We see worms on land when it rains. There are worms in oceans, too. The worms on the left are called feather-duster worms. They look just like the feather dusters people once used for cleaning furniture. The worms below are fire worms. Their bristles cause burning pain when touched. The bristles help protect fire worms from predators.

X x X x X x X x X x X x X x X x X x

Xmas tree worms

Christmas tree worms look like Christmas trees, which is how they got their name. Christmas tree worms live in the hard tubes at their centers. Their tentacles come out of the tubes to grab food. In a flash, the worms can again pull the tentacles into the tubes.

Christmas tree worms live on coral reefs.

What are these worms called? (See page 28.)

coral

You are an ocean!

Did you know that you have an ocean inside you? Your body is about three-quarters water. Three-quarters of the Earth's surface is covered by water, too. Ocean water is salty. If you have ever tasted your tears, you know they are also salty. You are a water creature living on a watery planet!

Zones of the ocean

People who study oceans divide them into **zones**, or areas. The image on this page shows how much sunlight each ocean zone receives. As the water gets deeper, there is less light. Different animals live in each zone. Plants and most animals can live only in the sunlit zone. This top zone is warmer and brighter than the other zones are.

The top zone of the ocean is the **sunlit zone**. Most ocean animals live here.

Very little light reaches the **twilight zone**. The water here is cold.

The **midnight zone** is completely dark. The temperature is just above freezing.

A a B b C c D d E e F f G g H h
Glossary

Note: Some boldfaced words are defined where they appear in the book.

backbone A series of bones that starts at the head and runs down the back

calf A young whale or dolphin

camouflaged Describing an animal's natural shape or coloring that allows it to blend in with its surroundings

coral reef An area in shallow ocean water that was formed from dead corals

equator An imaginary line drawn around the center of the Earth through areas that have hot temperatures year round

lava Red, hot, melted rock that pours from a volcano

mammal An animal with some hair or fur, a backbone, and which breathes air and drinks its mother's milk as a baby

population The total number of a certain animal in an area or on Earth

reptile An animal with a backbone, cold blood, and scaly skin; alligators, crocodiles, snakes, lizards, and turtles are reptiles

scales Small bony parts that protect the skin of fish and reptiles

tide The rising and falling of ocean water

tide pool Water trapped between rocks at seashores during low tide

top predator A big predator, such as a shark, that is not hunted by other animals

volcano A cone-shaped mountain with an opening through which hot lava and gases pour or shoot out

zone An area of land or ocean that has a certain purpose

Index

Printed in the U.S.A.